a pocketful of
RHYME
Imagination for a new generation

2006 Poetry Competition for 7-11 year-olds

YoungWriters

Verses From Leicestershire
Edited by Allison Dowse & Mark Richardson

 Young **Writers**

First published in Great Britain in 2007 by:
Young Writers
Remus House
Coltsfoot Drive
Peterborough
PE2 9JX
Telephone: 01733 890066
Website: www.youngwriters.co.uk

SB ISBN 978-1 84602 782 6

Foreword

Young Writers was established in 1991 and has been passionately devoted to the promotion of reading and writing in children and young adults ever since. The quest continues today. Young Writers remains as committed to the nurturing of poetic and literary talent as ever.

This year's Young Writers competition has proven as vibrant and dynamic as ever and we are delighted to present a showcase of the best poetry from across the UK and in some cases overseas. Each poem has been selected from a wealth of *A Pocketful Of Rhyme* entries before ultimately being published in this, our fourteenth primary school poetry series.

Once again, we have been supremely impressed by the overall quality of the entries we have received. The imagination, energy and creativity which has gone into each young writer's entry made choosing the poems a challenging and often difficult but ultimately hugely rewarding task - the general high standard of the work submitted ensured this opportunity to bring their poetry to a larger appreciative audience.

We sincerely hope you are pleased with this final collection and that you will enjoy *A Pocketful Of Rhyme Verses From Leicestershire* for many years to come.

Contents

Empingham CE Primary School

Humberstone Junior School

Aireena Amroota (10) 32
Megan Gibbons (10) 32
Mayaba Hapenga (11) 33
Hamza Cato (10) 34

John Wycliffe Primary School

Katie Davies (10) 34
Jack Sykes (8) 35
Reece Hutchings (9) 35
Bethany King (8) 36
Charlotte Turpin-Brown (8) 36
Olivia Ash 37
Emily Reed (8) 37
Maisie Greaves (9) 38
Max Pardoe (8) 39
Charlotte Hull (8) 40
Bryony Findley (9) 40
Rachael Malin (9) 41
Hannah Gmerek (8) 41
Mikela Gilmore (8) 42
Bryani Moulds (9) 42
Georgia Weston (9) 43
Charlotte Hill (7) 43
Debra Gower (8) 44
Abi Clarke (10) 44
George Austin (9) 45
Suthida Lathong (9) 45
George Macintyre 46
Anabel Dunn-Birch (6) 46
Hannah Roberts (9) 47
Ben White (9) 47
Elliot Michell (10) 48
Luke Hayward (7) 48
Jade Bradley (10) 49
Jessica Scott (11) 50
Georgia Lilley (10) 51
Morgan Machin (9) 51

Leighfield Primary School

Corinne Broughton (8) 52
Charlie Dawson (10) 52

Louisa Newell & Megan Wright (9)   74
Daniel Webster & Max Collins (9)   74
Rebecca Higley & Calypso Keightley (9)   74
Natasha Petty (10)   75

Mellor Community School

Roshni Makwana (9)   75
Raeesa Hussein (9)   76
Bijal Chauhan (10)   76
Anesu Rupango (9)   77
Zahra Mussa (9)   77
Ameyah Nugent (8)   78
Anika Bhardwa (8)   78
Sahil Dattani (8)   79
Ikra Omar (8)   80
Hiten Patel (8)   80
Rahul Somia (9)   81
Pratiksha Patel (9)   81
Neel Somaiya (9)   82
Umaimah Mussa (8)   82
Aamir Nur (8)   83
Hamzah Adam (8)   83
Maya Mistry (8)   83

New Swannington Primary School

Siobhan Robinson (9)   84
Emily Rudin (9)   84
James Payne (9)   84
Rhys Butler (9)   85
Kieran Briers (9)   85
Tania Bodle (10)   85
Jacob Coley (9)   86
Jordan Lester (9)   86
Sarah Thomas (9)   86
Sean Lynn (10)   87
Libby Birt (10) & Katie White (9)   87
Lydia Pollard (9)   87
Bethany Tatham (9)   88
Bethany Clarke (10)   88
Toby White (10)   88
Kia Storer & Elise Baxter (9)   89

Joshua Culpin (9)	89
Jamie Kerr (10)	89
Amelia Cayless (10)	90
Joseph Cayless (9)	90
Sam Moore (10)	91
Sophie Adkins (9)	91
Hannah Kelly (10)	92
Kieran Ridgway & Jordan Wayte (9)	92
Chloe Wesley (10)	93
Ty Wardle (10)	93
Rebecca Knight (10)	94
Mia Thompson (10)	94
Jasmin Edwards (10)	95
Luke Atkinson (10)	95
Brigitte Taylor (10)	96
Victoria Campbell (10)	96
Katie Wickham (10)	97
Charlie Stringer (10)	97
Callan Scott (10)	98
Maddi-Rose Harrison (11)	98
Demi Demetriou (11)	99
Amy Tebbatt (10)	99
Enola Curran (10)	100
Ellie Summers (10)	100
Lucy Wood (9)	101

The Poems

Recipe For A Holiday

Ingredients:

A teaspoon of happiness,
A bright white fluffy cloud,
A jam-packed suitcase,
A freezing cold drop of snow,
The most sun you've ever had,
Just one box of laughter,
A bright yellow sunset,
And one pure box of friends and family.

Method:

Assemble in any way you want for your happy holiday this year!

James Hackett (10)
Abington High School

Twins

I'm her and she's me,
We live in the same family.
They always get confused,
We don't get amused.
When it's bright and sunny,
We look the same and it's funny.

Brittany Limmage (10)
Abington High School

Twins

T wo of me,
W hat can you see?
I am she and she is me.
N ever three, just two you see!

Jordanna Limmage (10)
Abington High School

You're As Lonely

You're as lonely
as a piglet without its mother
as a child left to survive on its own
as a doll dropped in the rain
as a poster on the floor.

You're as lonely
as a hamster in its cage on its own
as a teacher without children
as a dog locked inside a car
as a head with no hat on it.

You're as lonely
as a dog with no owner
as a woman with no house
as a tree with no leaves
as a car with no keys.

You're as lonely
as a reindeer with no flight
as a Rudolph with no red nose
as a dad that can't shoot
as a mouse with no sight.

Louanna Fairbrother (11)
Abington High School

Acrostic Poem

A ll great players,
R eally fantastic,
S coring every game.
E ven playing away.
N ever losing a match,
A ll over the opposition,
L oving winning every game.

Bradley Hughes (10)
Abington High School

The Simile Poem

(Based on 'The Writer of this Poem' by Roger McGough)

The writer of this poem
is as strong as a giant
he can fix bikes
and he's a man reliant.

He's as fierce as a dog
but as quiet as a cat
he wears a nice pair of trousers
but an ugly, torn hat.

His face is handsome
his hat style is great
he wears a nice pair of trainers
but his socks are out of date.

The writer's best ever hobby is bikes
he works from morning to midday
which means he gets a good bike
and he doesn't have to pay.

Ryan Palmer (10)
Abington High School

Snowflakes

S oftly they fall in the night,
N ever floating, just falling,
O ver the houses and on top of trees,
W hite and soft like a feather
F alling, falling to the ground,
L ying like a blanket on the ground,
A ll around, the snow is everywhere,
K ind and gentle like a cloud,
E scaping across the land,
S leeping on the ground.

Tamsin Fisher (11)
Abington High School

You Are As Funny . . .

As a lion that doesn't like cubs
as a monkey that likes to visit pubs
as a slow runner that's a cheetah
as a clown that doesn't like people called Peter

You're as funny
as a snake with hot blood
as an elephant stuck in mud
as a bell that doesn't make the noise, *ding, dong*
as a teacher called Mr or Mrs Ping Pong

You're as funny
as a library without one book
as a cooker that doesn't cook
as a bucket without a hole
as a fireplace that has no coal

You're as funny
as a dog that has human years
as a rabbit that does not have ears
as a kangaroo that cannot bounce
as a tiger that is scared to pounce.

Louis Samuels (11)
Abington High School

The Mighty Num

He's ginger and fluffy
With a tail all a-bush
With ears that prick up
When it's time for a nosh.

Four legs he has,
One in each corner
What is he?
He's the Mighty Num.

Lauren Whittaker (10)
Abington High School

Little Machine

I'm a little washing machine,
chugging away,
twirling, whirling, whizzing all day.
I spin and whirl
until I can't twirl anymore.
Then you fill me up
and forget to close my door!

Spinning and twirling is my chore,
you think you don't like me,
because I roar.
You clean me carefully,
you always hurt my jaw.
Opening and closing
my metal door.

Megan Cooper (10)
Abington High School

Impossible

Not everything in the world is impossible,
Except you can't chop a metal table in half
Well I guess some things are,
Like throwing a car to touch a star,

Impossible

You can't chop your hand off without bleeding,
You will definitely hurt someone when speeding
A baby can't speak as soon as it's born
You won't get a bird out of frogspawn!

Impossible

You can't bend a metal pole,
A ball is bound to roll,
Humans can't fly,
Up high in the sky

Impossible!

Matthew Hruszka (10)
Abington High School

Stop That Door

I go to bed every night,
And try to get to sleep,
But the door disagrees with me,
He claps his hands,
Taps his feet,
Does a jiggle,
And grinds his teeth.
I locked the door,
So he wouldn't slam,
But now he rattles,
Singing, bang, bang, bang!

I phoned the woodcutter,
Told him the tale,
He wouldn't believe me,
So he put me in jail.
I'm free from the door,
No banging anymore.
When I got home,
From six months in jail,
There was the door,
Lonely and frail.

Chelsea Hougham (10)
Abington High School

The Rabbit And The Fox

The rabbit was happy,
And hopping around,
Until a fox appeared
From out of the ground,
The rabbit was scared and running around,
The fox ran and ran to catch the rabbit,
Children were shouting, 'Run rabbit, run!'
And then they stopped in the sun.

Holly Hayes (11)
Abington High School

Fog Is My Name

I shudder through the daylight,
Hugging everything around me,
Fog is my name.
All around me it's blurry,
Nothing to see,
Gloomy and dark,
People say, 'Who is this person?'
Fog is my name!
Now I'm dying,
I shiver with pain,
Everything is clear,
Where have I gone?
I have no idea.
Fog was my name.

Charlie Johnson (10)
Abington High School

Mirror

People come and stare,
Images beware.
You look at me,
I look at you.

Is this reflection
Real and true?
It's what's inside,
That I hide.

'Cause I'm a
Mirror personified!

Stephanie Mason (10)
Abington High School

The Sun And Me

I look up at the sun,
The sun looks down at me,
The sun's as hot as an oven,
Unlike me.

I smile up at the sun,
The sun smiles down at me,
The sun is as yellow as a lemon,
Not at all like me.

I laugh up at the sun,
The sun laughs down at me,
The sun's as round as an orange,
Unlike me.

Chloe Oliver (10)
Abington High School

The Wolf

W aiting for its prey,
O ften biting people when they are near it,
L urking around at night,
F rowning when it's a full moon.

Steffi Parker (10)
Abington High School

My Acrostic

B uzzing up and down
E ating and sucking pollen
E yes looking, but they don't want to come near me.

Bianca Elliott (10)
Abington High School

I Get Kicked All Day

I get kicked all day
I am a football.
I get kicked around all day,
I scream and scream,
But no one cares.
My legs are bruised, my body too,
And my head is very red.
My arms are cut,
From people's studs.
Oh, how I wish that they were me!
They'd never kick me round again,
And then I would be free.
Think of all the things I'd do,
If I wasn't me.

Lara Stomenov (10)
Abington High School

All About My Pet

I had a pet called Fred
Who a lump on his head
He was bright pink all over and very big
Guess what?
He was a fat, greedy pig!

Harvey Royle (10)
Abington High School

The Cat

C rouching on the mat
A t the moment she darts
T o her food.

Charmaine Barnes (10)
Abington High School

A Recipe For A Day Out

Ingredients:
1% touch of mardiness
99% touch of happiness
2 pints of sunshine
8 pints of slob
7 big cherries
I PSP

Method:
Take 1% of mardiness and sieve it in a bowl
Pinch 99% of happiness and add this to the bowl
Pour in 2 pints of sunshine
Add 8 pints of slob and whisk it by hand
Cut 7 big cherries and 1 PSP into cubes
Then mix them all together and your day is baked.

Adam Modan (10)
Abington High School

The Tree On The Hill

The tree on the hill stood, tall rough and strong,
With its dark brown trunk and green leaves,
Every day it would hope to not be cut down,
The tree and his friends fall down one by one,
Sadly the woodcutter cut it down and the tree died.

Lewis Johnson (10)
Abington High School

The Tree

It stood as tall as the Statue of Liberty,
And as round and sharp as the Leaning Tower of Pisa.
Brown at the bottom and green at the top, light in weight,
And it is proud of all these features.

Connor Watson (10)
Abington High School

Colourful

It has the shade of rose-pink
With bright blue eyes,
Which open at the break of dawn,
Cherry-flavoured lipgloss,
Which is so glossy, like the moon,
With a very fast movement,
And in the shape of a rectangle,
So smooth to touch,
And with the scent of a rose.

Megan Richards (10)
Abington High School

Flame

His eyes bright with flame,
His face full of hate.
He blows about from house to house,
Causing panic and even death.
He comes in yellow and red,
Coming for the kill,
His bloody knives he carries back
Across into the night.

Ruby Hryniszak (10)
Abington High School

The Car

The car whizzed around the corner,
The car thrashed down the street,
The car is as red as sunset
The roof is as dark as night,
The wheels are as shiny as a necklace,
That's the car for me.

Bradley Cooke (10)
Abington High School

Recipe For An Angel

Put a spoonful of happiness.
Stir in some sweetness.
Sprinkle in some fairy dust.
Cut up some fluff from angel wings.
Add some pink glitter.
Mix together with an angel's heart.
Cover with angel wings.
Cook until it sparkles.
Pour into a warm mouth.
And in one day you will be an angel!

Jessica Holland & Hannah Harbidge (10)
Abington High School

My Cat, Spice

My cat, Spice is
As thick as a dog
Sleeps like a log

As brave as a fox
Hides in a cardboard box

As friendly as can be
Just like you and me.

Natasha Cropper (10)
Abington High School

Melted Chocolate

Warm and thick, yummy and brown,
Milky and it smells so good.
Can get sickly but I don't mind,
That is my favourite thing!

Ionie Gagin (10)
Abington High School

Recipe For A Dragon

Fill the bathtub with fire,
Take a spoonful of candle wax,
Stir in some shark's teeth,
Put some tails in,
Form some bat wings together,
Put four giant claws in some acid,
Stir all the recipe in the bathtub,
Also put in a beard if you want a bearded dragon,
In a week you will have a dragon.

Oliver Lucas-Hammersley (10)
Abington High School

Getting A Dog

As good looking as me,
My pet dog will be
As clever as a cat,
As quick as a cheetah,
As funny as a joker.
My dog can play poker!
As loud as a lion's roar,
My dog's teeth are sharper than a saw.

Thomas Page (10)
Abington High School

My 4-Year-Old Sis

As naughty as me!
As small as a chair!
As weird as a teacher!
As stupid as an ant!
Now that's my little sis!

William Atterbury (10)
Abington High School

My Mum

As soft as a kitten
As warm as a mitten
As beautiful as a rose
Like her cute button nose
As pretty as a peach
As calm as a beach
As happy as a cat
As daft as a bat
As small as an elf
Just like myself
My mum!

Ryan Wicks (10)
Abington High School

My Pet Dog

As cute as a baby monkey
As strong as an ox
Like a maggot in salt
Like a sausage on a plate
As stupid as a clown
As yappy as a Pekingese
A tail like a pencil
Lips like a washed T-shirt
A coat like gold.

Thomas Booth (10)
Abington High School

Magor

M y dad is in his lorry,
A nd on a dark and mysterious night,
G oing to Magor in Wales,
O ut like a light when he gets home,
R oaring in the morning.

Milan Vranjes (10)
Abington High School

The Tortoise

T hat green scaly thing
O pen dry land
R igid shell of the tortoise
T he old tortoise plods along
O ver the land he goes
I s he there? No one knows
S o he plods along in the bright blazing sun
E very day he goes to the sea.

Imogen Lee (9)
Abington High School

The Sun

She has a yellow face and always dresses bright,
Without her it would never be light.
She dresses up in yellows and always has a smile on her face,
She doesn't move day or night, she will never win a race.
Always happy, never sad,
Always good, never bad.
Everybody knows her, she's everybody's friend,
She will never drive you round the bend.

Chloe Rojahn (10)
Abington High School

Tiger

T he tiger is never to mess with.
I ts terrifying way of ripping through the jungle without a care
in the world.
G oing places faster than a fire spreading to wood.
E very animal bows down to the tiger.
R oaring is the tiger's way of getting messages to other animals.

Codie Smith (10)
Abington High School

The Hurricane

An angry warrior,
Throwing down his jagged spears,
Stomping away.
While whistling eerily off-key,
To a song long forgotten.

A grumbling, grey man,
With one blind eye,
Poking his stick everywhere,
Tapping and listening,
To an old, scratchy radio.

A bucking horse,
Neighing and throwing his rider,
Down, down, down,
Colliding with the Earth,
And sending sparks through the ground.

Isabella Mezzetti (11)
Abington High School

Recipe For A Holiday

Ingredients:
Bright, golden sand
Yellow, shining sun
Golden tan
Deep blue sea
Bright, rainbow-coloured clothes
Green and blue bucket and spade
All the medicines we might need
Pack my deckchair, red and white
Make sure my friends come, mine and yours.

Method:
Stir for a week
Leave in a hot place
Then come back and go to sleep.

Samuel Smith (10)
Abington High School

Recipe Poem - A Perfect Holiday

A suitcase full of clothes and wonderful surprises,
A cosy first class seat on a plane,
Some lovely roast dinner when you just get into the hotel,
Unpack and then go and look around the beautiful city,
Grab your swimming kit and dive into the pool,
Get your best clothes on and go and watch a movie or show,
Go back to your room and have a cosy night's sleep,
In the morning have a tasty fried breakfast,
Then go down to the beach and do some surfing,
Get a gigantic ice cream and eat it in the hot sun,
Go and do some shopping and get some new trainers,
Finally go back and get a big posh dinner,
Go down to the club for a drink,
Join the karaoke and have a song,
Then have another cosy night in bed,
Finally pack up again and get breakfast,
Get on the first class, beautiful plane,
Finally when you get home jump on the sofa,
Have dinner,
Then switch on the TV and watch EastEnders!

Thomas Randall (10)
Abington High School

Rain

A miserable face full of tears,
Moving quickly through the grey sky,
Running, running,
With a grey skirt and navy top,
She stops, opens her grey eyes,
And cries and cries.

Rachel Borrows (10)
Abington High School

Football

His head as round as the moon.
He can move at great speeds.
He can be stopped in his path.
He likes to fly high in the air.
But he usually spends most of his time on the floor.
He'll get an angry face when hit.
He has ragged cloths or a padded body.

Oliver Howard (11)
Abington High School

The Tiger

T amed animal in the zoo
I nteresting and fun
G asping when he tries to get out of the cage
E ntertaining people with his vicious personality
R oaring when he's angry.

Charlotte Thompson (10)
Abington High School

The Dolphin

D iving deep
O pen water all around them
L eaping under the red-hot sun
P laying down in the coral reef
H appily swimming around gracefully
I ntruding sharks swimming by
N othing scaring them.

April Trigg (11)
Abington High School

The Wind

The soft blow of a person sending a shiver down your spine,
Chasing after you, finding you wherever you go.
Moving swiftly in the bright blue sky,
His woolly coat flying in the breeze,
His face shining in the sun,
Suddenly he turns angry, a tornado appears over the horizon,
Destroying everything in his way,
As night falls he calms down and everything is still.

Simran Gill (10)
Abington High School

Bengal Tiger

T iger, the biggest cat
I ncredibly ferocious
G rand hunters of the plain
E nergetic animals
R avenous at times.

Macauley Roberts (11)
Abington High School

The Stars

Like flickering light bulb,
A tiny dot up in the dark, twinkling sky,
Like a cheery, proud face,
With a happy personality,
Like a torch lighting up the moonlit sky,
A faraway rich and miraculously glamorous lady,
Who likes to go to lots of discos.

Amber Flude (10)
Abington High School

The Sun

It keeps moving through the sky,
A big ball of gas and fire,
A gorgeous smiling face,
Sometimes playing hide-and-seek,
Only hiding behind the clouds.
Bright yellow face,
Flaming golden hair,
Dressed in royal gold robes,
And shining slippers with brilliant jewels.
Then at night it goes to sleep,
In a curved chair,
After that it turns white,
To save its light.

Kate Greengrass (10)
Abington High School

Recipe For A Holiday

Ingredients
Nice, bright hot sun.
Sandy beach, hot in the sun.
Nice, calm sea waving along.
Family and friends full of laughter and fun.
Fishes in the sea swimming along.
A long pier out in the sea to go fishing from,
From dawn to dusk.

Method
Simmer and stir until it bubbles,
Put in the freezer until it's all together
And drop into Portugal for a week.

Peter Folwell (11)
Abington High School

A Recipe For A Holiday

Ingredients
Thin, bright, colourful clothes,
Sea is colossal and freezing.
Sun is gleaming, golden like a dandelion,
Sand is crispy, baking hot.
Friends running, jumping, having fun,
Family smiling, relaxed in the sand.
Cold crispy, delicious food,
Cosy, cold and warm caravan.

Method
Mix together however you want.
Place in 90° oven.
Stay there for three weeks.

Ayushi Pabari (10)
Abington High School

Superheroes

Superman can fly
Right up to the sky

Mr Fantastic is long
The Thing is strong

Batman can glide
Iceman will slide

The Hulk can bash
The Flash will dash

Superheroes are great
I wish I were their mate!

Danny Lewis (8)
Empingham CE Primary School

Thinking Of My Great Grandad

I saw it fall
Down on the wall
It was a bomb
I ran to mum
She said, 'Run
Into the bomb shelter!'

We were in there for days
Always
Looking out for Dad . . .

Lilli Frances Atkin (8)
Empingham CE Primary School

Dolphins

(Based on the poem 'Sea-Weed' by D H Lawrence)

Dolphins dance and dance and dart
as if dancing were their way of delaying
and if it drops on a rock it ducks
as dreamy people do.

Sarah Jones (9)
Empingham CE Primary School

Starfish

(Based on the poem 'Sea-Weed' by D H Lawrence)

Starfish slide and slide and slouch
As if sliding is their way of steadiness
And they stick to the silent seaweed
And over the slouching, slithering rocks.

Jessica Hayward (10)
Empingham CE Primary School

The Robin

I saw a robin hunting!
I saw a robin looking
At a worm
It landed carefully
It ate the worm
It flew back
Into the air
Then it shot back
To the nest.

Peter Gorringe (6)
Empingham CE Primary School

The Sea-Snakes

(Based on the poem 'Sea-weed' by D H Lawrence)

Sea-snakes slither and slither and slide
As if slithering was the form of stillness
And if it spots a fish
It will gobble and gobble away!

James Caine (10)
Empingham CE Primary School

Fox

It's got bright eyes that glow in the dark
Soft furry head that is very smooth
Black shiny whiskers
That's a fox!

Patrick Atkin (6)
Empingham CE Primary School

Dolls

I've got a doll called Annabell.
She sleeps in the pram while I visit Gran.
She is a good little doll,
And very slow.
When I go to Gran's I have a cup of tea,
Baby Annabell sits next to me.
She's very polite.
That's my doll.

Annie Hibbitt (6)
Empingham CE Primary School

Maths

Maths is my favourite subject,
Literacy and history, I slightly object,
Science is fun, I like to discover
About different things with my friends altogether.
But best of all I like adding and taking away,
Nearly as much as going out to play!

Jack Sharp (8)
Empingham CE Primary School

Conkers

Conkers are high up in the trees,
Conkers are high in a tree's eye,
Conkers are brown, falling from the sky.

Until a child comes and picks me up,
I'll wait on the ground looking all around.

That's a conker!

Tanya Davies (8)
Empingham CE Primary School

Cheetahs

Cheetahs are spotty.
Cheetahs are the fastest animals on the planet.
Cheetahs chase and kill the antelopes
And take them up trees to eat them.
Cheetahs are also known as hunting leopards.
Cheetahs have long tails and very sharp claws.
Cheetahs are orange and white with black spots.
Cheetahs live in the jungle.

Callum Archer (6)
Empingham CE Primary School

The Cat

Whiskers smooth and pointy
Eyes shiny, glowing and sharp
Head furry and soft
Tail wavy and stripy
Paws white and fluffy
That's a cat!

Emily Day (7)
Empingham CE Primary School

Maths

Maths, the subject I like best
I think it is better than all the rest
Numbers are everywhere, all around
Football scores, on front doors
They can always be found.

Oliver Dore (6)
Empingham CE Primary School

My Favourite Teacher

M aths teacher
I ncredible and cool
S uper teaching
S pecial in all ways

B eautiful
I n school she wears lovely clothes
D affodils and
D aisies are what she reminds me of
L ovely and kind
E nergetic and funny.

Nadine Katie Day (9)
Empingham CE Primary School

The Snake

Smooth, scaly, skin like some ribbon.
Small, soft head, like a ball.
Slimy, wet tongue like seaweed.
Sly, dangerous eyes like the Devil.
That's a snake!

George Hibbitt (8)
Empingham CE Primary School

The Fox

Foxes like eating chickens
Foxes eyes glow in the dark
Foxes ears can hear a mouse breathing
Foxes look for food in the moonlight.

Jamie Duggan (7)
Empingham CE Primary School

Autumn Leaves

I am a very proud leaf,
I am in my green summer coat,
I am proud of my coat,
We're all proud of our coats,
We feel great!

I have changed my coat,
To a lovely golden yellow!

I am a very proud leaf,
I am in my lovely golden yellow coat,
I am proud of my coat,
We're all proud of our coats,
We feel great!

I am a horrible brown leaf,
I am on my own now,
I'm hanging on to my tree,
I'm trying to stay on,
I'm moaning, crying, sobbing,
I'm lonely and angry,
I'm scared and upset,
I'm tired but can't sleep
Oh no, I let go!
I'm flying and falling,
Down
Down
Down
I'm touching the ground
I've *landed!*

Kayleigh Duke (10)
Humberstone Junior School

The Sly Fox

I'm a very sly fox, that's a fact,
With a very bristly tail that pats my back,
I am all alone with nothing to eat,
And I feel sharp pieces of glass on my feet,
But now I've found my mum, I'm nice and snug,
And I eat juicy bugs.
Even though at night-time, I will sneak out,
To walk very straight
But sometimes I pout,
Every now and then I smell people making food,
And when I see lights flicker,
It puts me in a good mood.
When people put food in the bin,
I always taste the chicken skin.
Every Tuesday when teenagers come out,
I always hear them yell and shout.

Laura-May Kaur Nahal (10)
Humberstone Junior School

The Terrifying Teachers

Who's the lady who
Teaches your lessons
And screams and shouts and takes away
All your favourite possessions?

At least now we don't have the cane
We would not be able to work
Because we would be in so much pain
The teacher would be to blame.

The teacher always gives us homework
I don't even have time to blink
Our brains are going to explode
Because we always have to think.

Aireena Amroota (10)
Humberstone Junior School

Forest Fire

Starting out as a little flame,
All pleasant and untamed,
Suddenly her size is growing,
She is why people are moaning,
Spreading fire, what to do
All these rumours are they true?
She is burning,
Until the morning,
She roars with life,
And causes strife,
She is happy that she lives,
After she destroys she gives.

Gavin Jones (10)
Humberstone Junior School

The Decaying Bike

I am a bike
Who was ridden once
He liked me to turn
And change gear a lot
But when he got a sparkling new bike
I was lonely for the very first time
But then one day
He came along
And took me out to have some fun
So then that day
I knew I was loved.

Joe Patterson (11)
Humberstone Junior School

The Star And The Tortoise

The slower I go the quicker I think,
I've got everything but the kitchen sink,
Up in my shell, that is my home, and I'm never alone,
I'm ninety-one and that is that,
I've been walking for a week and that's a fact,
My best friend is Lightning Hare,
Who wouldn't dare question luck,
On meeting my friend the star.
He twinkles up in the sky,
Until morning's nigh and leaves me by myself,
To travel the world.
He can shoot and spin and do everything,
Just like the sun but a lot more fun.
I can hear the frost being caught and told,
To not break any windows because it's so cold.
I can see the day turning into night,
What a beautiful sight.
I can smell some food,
Just drifting my way.
Preparing for another day,
When my star comes again, to travel the world.
He's already been to France,
And bought some pants,
Made from the finest silk,
They feel like honey and milk.
He has been to Italy,
But something tasted too bitterly,
You can hear stars colliding,
With one another, he is travelling the *world*.

Rebecca Link (10)
Humberstone Junior School

My Dream

I am a shoe,
Who has a dream,
I wish I were a runner's shoe,
I want to run and leap
With a runner.

But that's a dream,
I'm an old rag,
But I want to be a famous shoe,
I want to win gold, silver and bronze
With a runner.

Make more of me!
I want to be,
A fine laced one, with a Nike tick,
Silver tick or white tick,
And baby-blue.

I want to smell
The sandy tracks,
And all the hot dogs being sold,
And smell the dusty dust
That is in my way.

And hear the crowd,
Cheering for me,
As I enter the filthy track,
They scream and yell for me,
But that's just a dream!

Hannah Stephens (11)
Humberstone Junior School

The Amazing, Fabulous Dream Car

The car, the car
I have my own knowledgeable mind
Whenever I reverse
I don't look behind

When I turn on my engine
You can hear me talk
When you hear me break down
I pop like a cork

I break the speed limit
I go around town
I'm the best car in the world
I'm the *baddest* car around

My owners abandoned me
I feel so sad
Having no money
And going mad.

Aireena Amroota (10)
Humberstone Junior School

Personification Poem

Something is alive in the classroom
After the children go home
It isn't human, it's not the teacher or the children
And it isn't a dream.
The chair talks to the computer, happily,
Their conversation is hard to follow.

But then suddenly everything started to talk,
The ruler and pencil were having a fight
About who the children use more.
The computer and the chair shouted,
'Not again.'
And the ruler and the pencil stood still in silence.

Megan Gibbons (10)
Humberstone Junior School

Something

Something's happened
Something's started

Without the moon shining bright
Or the diamond's brilliant light
With the days getting shorter
And the nights even longer
With the shadows even scarier
And the days even murkier

Something's happened
Something's started

With the trees giving in
And dropping their gleaming gold
With their withering branches growing ever old
With the animals going to sleep
And the flowers dropping dead
Nature's at a stand still
Almost at the end

People are behaving like moles
Staying in their holes

Something's happened
Something's started
Winter's on the way
Just go, go away!

Mayaba Hapenga (11)
Humberstone Junior School

My Bruv The Bully

My brother is a bully,
He bullies me all day,
Especially in May, that's my birthday.

I gave him a slap,
I gave him a kick,
But still nothing happened to that twit.
So I hit him with a brick.
He fell to the floor, leaving a puddle of blood,
So I buried him in the mud.
The police found him the very next day,
They rushed him to hospital
On his birthday.

Hamza Cato (10)
Humberstone Junior School

Sea Dreaming

S un shining over the horizon of the crystal, glimmering water,
E ndless doughnuts oozing with sweet strawberry jam.
A iming for the sea with a smooth, stone-cold pebble.

D ripping from your toes in the sharp, cold, glassy water,
R ampaging across the sand to jump into the water
  as the tide pushes you away.
E dging away as the water chases you across the beach.
A nimals made from sand that take hours to make
  and seconds to destroy,
M iserable, (very rare at the sea), because you have
  no bucket and spade,
I mportant trip to the candy shop to buy a bar of sugary rock,
N ibbling away at the cornet that once held your favourite ice cream
G oing home is the worst bit, but look forward to the next trip.

Katie Davies (10)
John Wycliffe Primary School

The Weather

Water is strong,
Water does pong,
Water is a song,
Up into the sky.

Wind is clattering,
Wind is misty,
Wind is like cutlery,
Up into the sky.

Sun is a great big bun,
Sun is a pud,
Sun looks like blood,
Up into the sky.

Jack Sykes (8)
John Wycliffe Primary School

The Weather

The sun always cooks us,
It also makes a big fuss.
Why doesn't it catch a bus?
Early in the morning.

The snow is very cold,
Why won't it stop and hold?
Too bad it won't mould,
Early in the morning.

The weather is not great,
Too bad it delivers your fate,
The weather I always hate,
Early in the morning.

Reece Hutchings (9)
John Wycliffe Primary School

The Weather

The wind is whistling,
but the sun is glistening.
It goes for a wander,
as if it is fonder.
The wind is wild
like a naughty child.

Have you seen the sun?
it's not like a bun.
The sun is scorching.
when it is torching
The sun is so chilly,
is that really silly?

Have you heard of snow?
it is real you know.
When the snow is melting,
the rain is pelting.
My really big toe
does not like the snow.

Bethany King (8)
John Wycliffe Primary School

The Weather

The sun is shining down
On the trees
Sparkling on leaves.

The wind is blasting down
The debris is falling
On the hills.

The leaves are here
I can't see
I can't see the tree.

Charlotte Turpin-Brown (8)
John Wycliffe Primary School

The Weather

What shall we do with the horrible weather
What shall we do with the horrible weather
What shall we do with the horrible weather
Early in the morning?

Oh just look at that sun
Oops I shot a bird with a gun.
Oh I'd love a bun
Early in the morning.

Is it foggy outside?
Oh where is my doggy?
Why is it so soggy?
Early in the morning.

Why does it have to be freezing?
Could you stop that teasing?
I don't know who I'm pleasing,
Early in the morning.

What shall we do with the horrible weather
What shall we do with the horrible weather
What shall we do with the horrible weather
Early in the morning?

Olivia Ash
John Wycliffe Primary School

The Weather

What shall we do with the frightful weather
What shall we do with the frightful weather
What shall we do with the frightful weather
Early in the morning?

Make the dangerous lightning stop.
Make the wandering thunder drop.
Make the howling snow plop.
Early in the morning.

Emily Reed (8)
John Wycliffe Primary School

The Funny Weather

The wind is wild
like a screaming child.

The sound of thunder
makes me wonder.

Splashing in the rain
again and again.

Early in the morning.

The wind is whistling
while the sun is glistening.

The bright coloured sun
means I can have fun.

Today is chilly
and I'm being very silly.

Early in the morning.

The storm is terrifying
but it's flying.

I don't like it when it's foggy
because it makes me soggy.

When it is blistery
my clothes are flustery.

Early in the morning.

Maisie Greaves (9)
John Wycliffe Primary School

The Weather

What shall we do with the horrible weather
What shall we do with the horrible weather
What shall we do with the horrible weather
Early in the morning?

The sun is shining, the wind whining,
Sorry love, we weren't actually dining,
Early in the morning.

What shall we do with the horrible weather
What shall we do with the horrible weather
What shall we do with the horrible weather
Early in the morning?

It is so foggy
Where is my doggy?
I gave my doggy
A croggy.

What shall we do with the horrible weather
What shall we do with the horrible weather
What shall we do with the horrible weather
Early in the morning?

Max Pardoe (8)
John Wycliffe Primary School

The Weather

The sun is as bright as the world's first light.
The thunder gave me a fright as I was studying height.
The rain is scary in the night.
The weather is weird.

The wind is really wild,
The rain is becoming piled,
Today it is very mild.
The weather is weird.

Today the rain is really wet,
In fact it is soaking my pet.
And the wind is blowing
Around my boy's football net.
The weather is weird.

Charlotte Hull (8)
John Wycliffe Primary School

The Weather

Lightning flashes through the air,
Very loud it makes a cloud,
Babies screaming, very quiet,
Makes a dog go very wild.

Rain is blue and clear,
It falls from the sky,
It makes big puddles,
The children go and fly.

Wind is very windy,
It blows you round and round,
Leaves fall from the trees,
The wind goes down and down.

Bryony Findley (9)
John Wycliffe Primary School

The Weather

What shall we do with the horrible weather
What shall we do with the horrible weather
What shall we do with the horrible weather
Early in the morning?

Go home and have a cup of tea,
Make yourself a brand new key,
I slipped and hurt my knee
In this horrible weather.

Please make the sun come out,
Please make the sun come out,
Please make the sun come out,
Early in the morning.

As I walked down the street,
The sun glistened on my feet,
Then it started to sleet,
Early in the morning.

Rachael Malin (9)
John Wycliffe Primary School

The Weather

The sun is as bright as the stars at night,
And the thunder gave me a fright whilst I was studying light.
But the sun's also light so I have a sight.
Early in the night.

The wind made it foggy, so I couldn't see,
And my little doggy and me
Got as soggy as the sea.
Early in the night.

The wind can be misty, just like the sea,
And it can be very wise, like me
And my hand is very tired you see.
Early in the night.

Hannah Gmerek (8)
John Wycliffe Primary School

The Weather

The weather can be frightening,
Sometimes it can be lightning,
Sometimes it can be thundering,
And sometimes it can be blasting.

The weather can be sunny,
The weather can be runny,
Sometimes it can be foggy,
And sometimes it can be windy.

The weather can be frosty,
The weather can be misty,
Sometimes it can be scorching,
And sometimes it can be freezing.

The weather can be wondering,
The weather can be shivering,
Sometimes it can be whistling,
And sometimes it can be blazing.

Mikela Gilmore (8)
John Wycliffe Primary School

The Winter

It might be misty
and also frisky,
it also could be crystally.

The wind is also wandering,
it also could be thundering,
be careful, it could be crusty.

The weather is bad,
it could be mad,
sometimes it could be glad.

Bryani Moulds (9)
John Wycliffe Primary School

The Weather

What shall we do with this awful weather
What shall we do with this awful weather
What shall we do with this awful weather
Early in the morning?

Stop the horrible rain from falling,
Stop all the people from crying and bawling,
Because it is very stupid and appalling.
Early in the morning.

What shall we do with this awful weather
What shall we do with this awful weather
What shall we do with this awful weather
Early in the morning.

Please God we were only joking,
Ow, that hurts, stop your poking,
How come your ears are smoking,
Early in the morning?

Georgia Weston (9)
John Wycliffe Primary School

Legs, Legs And More Legs

Cat legs
Dog legs
Down legs
Skinny legs
Dad legs
Mum legs
Penguin legs
Bear legs
Clown legs.

Charlotte Hill (7)
John Wycliffe Primary School

The Weather

What shall we do with this frosty day
What shall we do with this frosty day
What shall we do with this frosty day
Early in the morning?

Stop it thundering and lightning,
Stop it whistling and blustering,
Stop it snowing and raining,
Early in the morning.

What shall we do with this frosty day
What shall we do with this frosty day
What shall we do with this frosty day
Early in the morning?

Stop the rain from falling,
Stop the snow from coming,
Stop the wind from blowing,
Early in the morning.

Debra Gower (8)
John Wycliffe Primary School

Cats

Lying around not knowing what to do,
Then suddenly it comes to you.

You plod outside,
The cat flap, then . . .
Pounce! You've caught him, like that.

He wriggles and squirms,
Until he gets free,
You look around to try to find him,
But you have no luck.

You go back to the stairs
And have a nice dream
Until the next day,
You'll find him again.

Abi Clarke (10)
John Wycliffe Primary School

Masoopa

Masoopa is gross
And he ran into a post
He's very thick
And likes to dress like a stick.

He had to escape
So he ran to the gate.
He wasn't so sure
So he slammed the door.

He got in his car
And ate a chocolate bar.
He drove away
And he drove into a lump of clay.

He reversed and went back
And he broke his back.
He went to the hospital
And they said it was impossible.

George Austin (9)
John Wycliffe Primary School

Alien Encounter - The Strange Alien Planet

Alien's planet
Freezing and cold
People are strange with three noses
Things are filled with lots of gold
Alien's gardens are filled with lost roses.

Alien's planet
Green and red
People have got eight legs
Aliens have got six heads
But I've never heard of aliens eating bread.

Suthida Lathong (9)
John Wycliffe Primary School

The Sun

He's an enormous star far above the sky,
He sparkles like a human wink, directly from the eye.

He sleeps at night, dozing off,
He wakes in the morning with a yawn and a cough.

He smells the blossom trees down on the Earth
And looks down at the green shimmering turf.

He looks at the church and hears the birds sing,
And stares at the flowers, all shiny, glimmering.

He looks at the children playing along,
And the jolly people singing their song.

Mothers embracing their children before school,
He looks at different trees, big and small.

Prosperous teenagers who passed GCSEs,
Old ladies eating cake and drinking their teas.

He smiles at everyone at the start of the day,
And lives a happy life, that's all I can say.

Some people think he's just a flaming rock in the sky,
But to most people he brings a tear to their eye.

George Macintyre
John Wycliffe Primary School

The Rabbits

Rabbits are cute,
Rabbits are small,
Rabbits are fast runners,
Rabbits are fluffy,
Rabbits are bouncy too.

Anabel Dunn-Birch (6)
John Wycliffe Primary School

The Whispering Wind

Make way he's coming,
You can hear him whizzing by,
He has come for his shopping
Everyone moves to the side.

As you walk to your art class,
You feel him brushing by you,
You feel like a picture,
And now he's painting you.

He turns your cookers on,
You smell burning from afar,
He's just like a ghost,
Whispering in the air.

You feel ecstatic as he ambles past you,
When you touch his hand you feel like a celebrity,
Walking down the red carpet.

Hannah Roberts (9)
John Wycliffe Primary School

Alien Encounter - Stupid

My alien is stupid
My alien is thick
My alien plays with a stick
My alien likes pick 'n' mix

My alien is tall and blue
My alien sits on the loo
My alien looks like a kangaroo
That's why he's called Roo

My alien plays football
But never gets a goal
He's better as a goalkeeper.

Ben White (9)
John Wycliffe Primary School

The Park

At the park, social life is at its summit
The busy squirrel's nest is covered, as he lays his nuts upon it
They hurriedly gather up nuts, chittering about the time
And the watchful trees in all their green lime.

The trees wave their arms as if out of mind
And the park keeper who is so kind
The playful puppies on the field, running to their owner
The mower's sound is like that of a bad moaner.

The flowers bloom, they smell so sweet
In the play area toddlers scuttle on clumsy feet
Cautious and wary the cat stalks its prey
The trees wave their branches to get in its way.

The trees wavy branches reach down like long hair
Children leap around like a jumpy hare
The ball goes into a tree, and the tree waves to dislodge it
The crowd cries out after that near hit.

Elliot Michell (10)
John Wycliffe Primary School

Alien Encounter - Zinog

Zinog is green
Zinog is scaly
Zinog can fly
Zinog keeps his skin soft by using lava
He can send messages though the air
He can write in different languages
His friends are Slime and Boop
He can electrocute things.

Luke Hayward (7)
John Wycliffe Primary School

Snow

Snow,
Bitter cold fingers
Touching you on the shoulders.

Snow,
Modest white stars
Falling from the sky.

Snow,
Hearing the little white stars
Gently fall to the ground.

Snow,
A clean-smelling aroma
Enriching the air.

Snow,
Tastes like plain, white, fluffy
Ice cream.

Snow,
Like miniature blobs of toothpaste
Landing on the bristly trees.

Snow,
Letting you know that
Winter is here.

Snow,
Bashing in to everything
She sees.

Snow,
The sun has risen
And the snow is disappearing into the air.

Jade Bradley (10)
John Wycliffe Primary School

A Spell From Shakespearean Times

(Inspired by 'Macbeth')

Watch the cauldron shine and glow,
Making sure it doesn't blow,
Rat that wiggles round the floor,
Bits of pig, we all adore,
Spiders wild and rotten hair,
The intestines of a bear.

'Double, double, toil and trouble,
Fire burn and cauldron bubble'.

Whiskers of a frightened cat,
The bristles of a muddy mat,
Eyes are yummy, 'specially frogs,
The wagging tail of a puppy dog,
The sticky paws of a child,
Chilli powder, extremely mild,
The sticky spit of a smelly camel,
The brain of a clever mammal.

'Double, double, toil and trouble,
Fire burn and cauldron bubble'.

A zebra's stripe, with a hoof,
Dear old Grandma Margaret's tooth,
A fish fin, baked on high,
A bright red robin from the sky,
A turkey wing from the yard,
A snail shell, almost rock hard,
For twenty minutes burn it well,
Two Devil horns from deep, dark Hell.

'Double, double, toil and trouble,
Fire burn and cauldron bubble'.

Mix it up as well as you can,
Put it in the frying pan.

Jessica Scott (11)
John Wycliffe Primary School

Alien Encounter - Blaster The Six-Legged Alien

My alien is called Blaster,
He is 7 years old,
He is a walking master,
And makes everyone very cold.
His legs get in our way,
They sometimes get stuck on us,
We tell throughout the day,
And we make such a fuss.

In the middle of the night,
He is very quiet,
But in the morning
He is a riot.

Even though he is a pain,
He can also be very nice,
He helps us in the kitchen,
But makes such a noise!
His legs can be very annoying,
They sometimes knock things over,
I wish he could be like us,
With two legs instead of 6.

Georgia Lilley (10)
John Wycliffe Primary School

Alien Encounter - Zapperdy Zog

Zapperdy Zog is coming,
Run and hide, we can hear him humming,
He will trash all our stuff, he's coming through the bush!
Close your windows, doors and gates; don't run, don't push.

Zapperdy Zog is a troubled little thing,
He looks for mischief.
His worst was the opera, when he sang,
So wherever you go, be careful, Zapperdy Zog is everywhere!

Morgan Machin (9)
John Wycliffe Primary School

Down By The Lakeside

Down by the lakeside
when the sun rises,
see all the ducks
some learning how to swim.

Down by the lakeside
at lunchtime,
see all the picnics and all
the families.

Down by the lakeside
when the sun sets,
everyone's gone home now
gone home to bed.

Down by the lakeside
when everyone's fast asleep,
here come the owls, the bats
and the beasts.

Corinne Broughton (8)
Leighfield Primary School

Winter

I can smell winter here, fresh
pine-scented leaves on the winter trees.
I can see winter is here, blankets of
snow covering patches of grass.
I can taste winter is hear, the cold, crisp
flakes of snow as they land on my tongue.

I can hear winter's here, feet scurrying
around buying presents.
I can feel winter's here, the warmth
from the log fire warming my hands.

Charlie Dawson (10)
Leighfield Primary School

When You're Not There

When you're not there I'm like . . .
Romans without Rome,
A queen without a throne,
Greeks without shields.
A farmer without his fields,
Protractors without angles,
Indians without bangles.
A dragon without its flare,
A ghost without its scare.
A Greek vase without clay,
A year without May.
Dogs without hair
Bad guys without lairs!

Christopher Chapman (10)
Leighfield Primary School

When You're Not There I'm Like . . .

A bull without horns
A cob without corn
A head without hair
A ghost without a scare
SATs without questions
A paper without sections
A door without a handle
Lunchtime without a scramble
Sausages without mash
A till without cash
Knights without shields
A farmer without fields
A food-fight without a mess
Bea without Tess.

Jack Mann (10)
Leighfield Primary School

When You're Not There

When you're not there I'm like . . .
Me with no candy,
Milly-Molly with no Mandy.
A mouse with no tail
Weather with no hail.
A chicken with no head,
Me without Greg,
Harry with no Ron.
A cymbal with no bong.
A calculator with no sum,
A baboon with no bum,
A skunk with no pong,
A singer with no song.
A bird with no nest,
A teacher with no test.
A hammer with no nail
A female with no male,
An apple with no pear,
A nit with no hair.
A story with no adventure,
Mr England with no long lecture,
Pan with no hook,
A cranny with no nook.
Honey with no bee,
Milk with no tea,
Pencil with no lead
Velma with no Fred.
The sun with no moon,
A mummy with no tomb.

Clara Feely (10)
Leighfield Primary School

When You're Not There

When you're not there, I'm like . . .
A cat without a purr,
A he without a her.
A foot without a sock,
A door without a lock.
A fireman without a fire,
An angel without a lyre.
Tessa without a flamingo,
A granny without bingo.
A wizard without a spell,
A devil without Hell.
One without two,
A bathroom without a loo.
A question without an answer,
A dance without a dancer.
X-Factor without Simon Cowell,
A wolf without its howl.
A finger without a nail,
Bart Simpson without a fail.
A mum without a dad,
A young lady without a lad.
A lounge without a vase,
An alien without Mars.
A postman without mail,
A storm without hail.
A girl without a phone,
A teenager without a moan.
A laugh without a hee, hee,
My family without me!

Tessa Cooper (10)
Leighfield Primary School

When You're Not Here,

I'm like . . .
A snake with no hiss,
A girl without her kiss.
A kangaroo with no bounce,
A lion with no pounce,
A foot with no sock,
A clock with no tock,
A horse with no jump,
A camel with no hump.
A dragon with no flight,
A giant with no height.
A shark with no teeth,
A tree with no leaf.
A birthday with no cake,
A garden with no rake.
A sink with no tap,
A traveller with no map.
Some paint with no brush,
A wind with no gush,
Dracula with no lair,
A human with no air.

Lilly Hives (10)
Leighfield Primary School

Hurricane

I can kill people by spinning them and by
throwing them down,
I can go a thousand miles an hour and
pick up churches with one swift gust.

I can go in the sea and disappear as
quickly as I came.

When I am angry, don't get in my way.

Robbie McCall (8)
Leighfield Primary School

Animal Magnetism

I'm as attracted to you as pen to paper.
I'm as attracted to you as Mum's to 'Later.'

I'm as attracted to you as a dog to a bone.
I'm as attracted to you as a girl to a phone.

I'm as attracted to you as a computer to a game.
I'm as attracted to you as an actor to fame.

I'm as attracted to you as a writer to a book.
I'm as attracted to you as a fish to a hook.

I'm as attracted to you as a monkey to cheek.
I'm as attracted to you as Mrs M to the Ancient Greeks.

I'm as attracted to you as me to ham.
I'm as attracted to you as Tilly to lamb.

I'm as attracted to you as vampires to blood.
I'm as attracted to you as pigs to mud.

I'm as attracted to you as a pencil to a sharpener.
I'm as attracted to you as wood to a carpenter.

I'm as attracted to you as a dragon to its teeth.
I'm as attracted to you as a tree to a leaf.

I'm as attracted to you as a cook to food.
I'm as attracted to you as painters to nudes.

Elliot Prior (10)
Leighfield Primary School

The Eagle

I glide in the distance,
I am dangerous, quick and quiet.

I can be vicious when enemies are near
But I can be silent when I hear or see my prey.
I sweep down freely to get my prey and glide
                                    proudly to my home.
Back to my chicks, then rest again.

Jack Morris (8)
Leighfield Primary School

Without You!

When you're not there, I'm like . . .

Sweetcorn without a cob,
My sister without a sob.

Wool without a sheep,
A kangaroo without a leap.

A mouse without cheese,
A dog without fleas.

Food without a gut,
A Zulu without a hut.

Me without a PC,
A leg without a knee.

Alfie without Bob,
Christians without God.

I'm sad and blue
When I'm not with you.

Jamie Gregory (10)
Leighfield Primary School

When You're Not There

I'm like
A rabbit with no hop
A farmer with no crop
A hare with no hair
A boy without his bear
A mouse without cheese
A world without bees
A chicken without his pen
Ben without his den
Guy without 'Doctor Who'
Aliens with no goo
A sea with no harbour
A test without getting harder.

Gavin Wood (11)
Leighfield Primary School

The Wind

The wind is a transparent ghost
Slipping through the sky
Howling in its high-pitched notes
Swooping from up high.
The ghost is soaring through the air
Wailing, letting out a cry.

And when it becomes night
Still it never stops
Crashing against windows
Sailing past the rooftops.
Everyone's asleep in bed
Then finally it drops.

It finally comes to rest
Going to its post
Waiting for another time
When it's needed most.

Benjamin Hickman (10)
Leighfield Primary School

Silent Things

A mouse tiptoeing across the floor,
A thesaurus waiting to be used,
A tortoise crawling across the sand,
A lion waiting to pounce,
My milk chocolate-brown teddy bear
Waiting to be cuddled.
A spicy chilli waiting to be eaten,
Trapped in the fridge.

Lydia Grice (8)
Leighfield Primary School

When You're Not There, I'm Like . . .

A pig with no mud.
A flower with no bud.
A volcano with no lava.
A human with no father.
A mouse without cheese.
A mum without keys.
A scorpion without a sting.
A queen without her king.
A cow without milk.
A dress without silk.
A church without a bell.
A water without a well.
Amelia without swimming.
A stone without skimming.
An elephant without a trunk.
A biscuit without a dunk.
Mrs M without Greeks.
Birds without beaks.
Tigers without a prowl.
Lions without a growl.
Snakes without a hiss.
Bedtimes without a kiss.
A mouth without a tongue.
Me without my mum.

Cody Thorndyke-Andrew (10)
Leighfield Primary School

Silent Things

My hamster drifting off to sleep,
Green Christmas tree, waiting to be used.
Perfect piece of paper ready to be written on,
A crisp trying to get out of its packet.
A tree waving goodbye,
Spiders making their webs.

Jemima Feely (8)
Leighfield Primary School

Winter

I can feel winter's here
when I go outside.
A gust of cold air,
freezing, bitter and biting.

I can see winter's here
when I look out my window.
Trees, bare of leaves,
snowflakes drifting from the sky.

I can hear winter's here
when the geese fly over.
Calling to each over,
flying to Rutland Water.

I can taste winter's here
when I drink my hot chocolate.
Or eat nice hot soup
which is warming and comforting.

Louis George (10)
Leighfield Primary School

Oak Tree

I am old, silent, generous and thoughtful,
I house rabbits, squirrels and many more.
My enemies are woodcutters and lumberjacks.

I give acorns to children or can be a goalpost
Lightsaber, a climbing frame or simply a hiding place.
My clothes are wood and leaves and my bark is as smooth as silk.

My grandchildren grow all around me,
We stay together through sun, heat, snow, rain and time.

David Cunnington (9)
Leighfield Primary School

Animal Magnetism

I'm as attracted to you as a pupil to learning
I'm as attracted to you as a fire to burning.
I'm as attracted to you as a teacher to his class
I'm attracted to you as a window cleaner to glass.
I'm as attracted to you as a dog to a bark
I'm as attracted to you as a toddler to a park.
I'm as attracted to you as a tenor to singing
I'm as attracted to you as an athlete to winning.
I'm as attracted to you as a pig to muck,
I'm as attracted to you as bread to a duck.
I'm as attracted to you as a writer to a pen
I'm as attracted to you as a wolf to his den.
I'm as attracted to you as a chef to cooking
I'm as attracted to you as a boss to booking.
I'm as attracted to you as a king to looking smart,
I'm as attracted to you as a painter to art.
I'm as attracted to you as a roof to a light,
I'm as attracted to you as a child to a kite.
I'm as attracted to you as a baby to baths.
I'm as attracted to you as an engineer to maths.

Benjamin Allen (11)
Leighfield Primary School

Silent Things

Germs spreading,
Hair cuddling my head,
A letter box opening its mouth,
A tree waving its branch,
Electricity passing through a wire,
Tortoises nibbling some lettuce.

Dominic Hickman (8)
Leighfield Primary School

When You're Not There

When you're not there
It's like . . .
Some paper with no pen,
An egg with no hen,
A window with no glass,
A field with no grass,
A foot with no shoe,
A bathroom with no loo,
A tap with no water,
A pizza with no quarter,
A library with no books,
A picture with no hook,
A theatre with no chairs,
A wood with no bears,
A clock with no hands,
A kitchen with no pans,
A room with no lights,
A cliff with no height,
A door with no mats,
A bin with no cat.

Rhys Burton (11)
Leighfield Primary School

The Sea

I can eat you up and lift up boats.
I can sweep the shore, make ducks float,
                              or swallow ships up.
When I am happy, I dance like a ballerina,
When I am angry, I roar like a lion.

Lydia Thompson-O'Connor (8)
Leighfield Primary School

The Wind

I am powerful and strong,
I can feel the heat and the cold.
I am energetic and my power is endless.
But on a sunny day, I don't destroy,
I relax and I can feel the clouds floating through me.
I can see the world glistening in the sun,
When I am joyful, I dance and swirl.

Angus Cooper (8)
Leighfield Primary School

Sea

In my depths I see gleaming treasure sinking into my calm sand
with creatures crawling on top.
I can feel boats bobbing up and down on my head and drifting
away peacefully.
When people drop litter on my watery coat I get vicious and angry,
welling up and crashing my water.
When I am angry I kill people with my deadly waves.

Megan Thompson-O'Connor (8)
Leighfield Primary School

Hurricane

I can destroy warehouses, airports or just carrots in a field,
I can lift up skyscrapers and lift up ants.
Or make a noise without opening my mouth.
When I am tired, I will go away, but I will return in days or months.

Tim Stuart (8)
Leighfield Primary School

Animal Magnetism

I'm as attracted to you as a pen to writing.
I'm as attracted to you as a bear to biting.
I'm as attracted to you as bubble to gum.
I'm as attracted to you as a cherry to a bun.
I'm as attracted to you as a dog to a bone.
I'm as attracted to you as ice cream to a cone.
I'm as attracted to you as a swan to water.
I'm as attracted to you as a brick to mortar.
I'm as attracted to you as scissors to cutting.
I'm as attracted to you as a man to hunting.
I'm as attracted to you as a cow to a calf.
I'm as attracted to you as a clown to a laugh.
I'm as attracted to you as a chick to an egg.
I'm as attracted to you as clothes to a peg.

Charlotte Copperthwaite (10)
Leighfield Primary School

Sea

I can smash the boats and eat the wood,
I can fight the rocks and splash the children
Or tickle their feet.
When I am angry, I eat boat sandwiches.

William Hathaway (8)
Leighfield Primary School

Sea

I can feel fish scattering and slipping on me,
I can lift boats up to make me laugh
Or I can be vicious and nasty.
I can be grumpy to everyone,
When I am sleepy, I can be silent.

Grace Chapman (8)
Leighfield Primary School

Winter's Here

I can see that winter's here.
Floating snowflakes falling to the ground.
Frost clings to leafless branches.

I can taste that winter's here.
Roasting goose sizzling in the oven.
Jacket potatoes crisping in their skins.

I can feel that winter's here.
Hands numbing in the icy cold.
Icy ears tucked inside hats.

I can smell that winter's here.
Fruity Christmas cake cooking in the oven.
The smell of pine needles falling off the trees.

I can hear that winter's here.
Carol singers laughing at the door.
The shake of sleigh bells.

Alastair Lewis (10)
Leighfield Primary School

Silent Things

A car rusting
Hares running,
Ewes grazing,
A tractor left in a field,
A deserted house,
Butter trapped in a fridge.

Hector Thorne (8)
Leighfield Primary School

Winter

I can see that winter's here,
Robin red breast hopping in the garden,
Presents under the Christmas tree.

I can feel that winter's here,
The flickering fire warming my hands
The feel of the snow going through my gloves.

I can smell that winter's here,
The lovely turkey roasting in the oven,
The scent of the pine needles on the Christmas tree.

I can hear that winter's here,
Cracking the Christmas cracker,
Ripping the wrapping paper.

I can taste that winter's here,
Eating the Christmas dinner,
The delicious mince pie and cream.

Abigail Aleixo (10)
Leighfield Primary School

Silent Things

Silent ants under the carpet
A leaf just about to fall,
Some people tiptoeing across the hall.
Fresh lettuce trapped in the fridge
Dew dripping off the leaves
Flies laying their eggs.

Jason Mann (8)
Leighfield Primary School

Spring

I can hear that spring is here,
Birds chirping in the treetops,
The soft breeze blowing my hair.

I can see that spring is here,
The new flowers peeking up from the ground.
The sun gazing brightly between the clouds.

I can feel that spring is here,
The rain on my skin.
The fresh air rushing past me.

I can taste that spring is here,
The savoury taste of apple pie and
Custard and home-made pancakes
With syrup, rising in the frying pan.

I can smell that spring is here,
The freshly cut grass.
The mid-morning rain on the newly grown grass.

Charlotte Bolton (10)
Leighfield Primary School

Spring

I can hear that spring is here . . .
Sweet singing of the birds and the first cuckoo.

I can see that spring is here . . .
Daffodils in the breeze and trees full of blossom.

I can smell that spring is here . . .
Mowed grass and delicate spring flowers.

I can taste that spring is here . . .
Delicious chocolate Easter eggs and newly dug potatoes.

I can feel that spring is here . . .
cuddly baby lambs and fluffy spring chicks.

Beatrice Flavell (10)
Leighfield Primary School

Animal Magnetism

I'm as attracted to you as leaves to trees.
I'm as attracted to you as buzz to bees.
I'm as attracted to you as my mum to a car.
I'm as attracted to you as my dad to a bar.
I'm as attracted to you as football to a guy
I'm as attracted to you as me to a pie.
I'm as attracted to you as food to a cook.
I'm as attracted to you as my sister to a book.
I'm as attracted to you as mountains to peaks.
I'm as attracted to you as knowledge to Greeks.
I'm as attracted to you as a girl to a phone.
I'm as attracted to you as a dog to a bone.

Ben Lawton (10)
Leighfield Primary School

The Wind

The wind is a gliding bird
Swooping through the sky
It falls down avoiding the ground
Then moans and wails in its flight
It batters against the grass,
Then shoots back up to fly.

It turns around, enjoying itself,
Then splashes into the water
When it comes out, it blasts into the air.

As night comes, it goes slower,
It gently glides across the horizon
Then drifts down and falls asleep
Until it has gone, tomorrow it will come back!

Amanda Hemmings (10)
Leighfield Primary School

A Stream

A stream is a stealthy snake,
Slithery and shiny,
Making its way through the muddy banks,
Travelling to different places.
Hissing slightly while it slides over rocks,
Gobbling its innocent prey,
Constantly night and day,
As it sprints past you,
There is a gasp of fright.

Curving and swerving
Left and right.
Going through towns when it's no longer light,
It slinks round a bend . . . then *wow!*
Racing down a steep slope,
It gains control when it gets to the bottom,
But still goes rushing, sprinting, racing past.

Night comes creeping up,
And at last it slows down,
Winding its way back to its den,
Ignoring the passing women and men.

Amelia Grice (10)
Leighfield Primary School

Kennings

Meat savager
Food scoffer
Fast eater
Swift swimmer
Bone shatterer
Good disguiser
River owner
Fast snapper.

Craig Roberts (10)
Leighfield Primary School

The Wind

The wind is a howling wolf,
Growling in my face,
He whines and wails when he wants to play,
He prowls from place to place.

The wolf bounds through the sky,
Down low and up high,
He slinks around the fluffy clouds,
Playing hide-and-seek.

At night when it's all quiet,
He creeps back to his den,
Then . . .
        Sleeps.

Alice Buzzard (10)
Leighfield Primary School

Zoo Friendship

As the elephant reaches for your hand,
He really wants to touch your heart,
If the giraffe reaches his neck up high,
He can see the birds flying in the sky.

When the rhino sees his friends eating,
He asks them if he can join,
And when they say yes,
He sits down for a rest
And he eats away all day.

When the penguins waddle in the water
They meet all their friends.

Abigail Thompson-O'Connor (9)
Leighfield Primary School

Paw Prints

Paw prints, paw prints are the best.
They walk around dripping wet.
Little doggies run around
Making paw prints on the ground.

Furry kittens on the ground
Making paw prints all around.
Big strong cats stroll around
Making paw prints round and round.

Cats and dogs huddle round
After a long day out and around.
Sleepy sleepy they are now
Goodnight paw prints, go to sleep now.

Henrietta Teasdale-Brown & Sabrina Lucas (9)
Leighfield Primary School

Christmas Eve

Christmas Eve is very exciting,
Waiting for Santa to come,
You'd better try and get some sleep,
Tomorrow's going to be fun!

Presents wrapped in silver paper,
Crumpled on the floor,
I hope I get my favourite toy!
My sack's hung on the door!

Christmas dinner is the best
The lovely turkey leg,
I can't wait for my dessert!
I got my toy, I called it Meg!

Lauren Rootham (10)
Leighfield Primary School

Summer

I can hear that summer's here.
Children screaming in the park,
The jingling of my Coca-Cola.

I can see that summer's here.
Athletes in sleeveless tops,
Burnt sausages on the barbecue.

I can taste that summer's here.
Dark red strawberries and cream,
Pimms, fresh from the jug.

I can smell that summer's here.
Bright red roses waft,
Flames from the outside grill.

I can feel that summer's here,
Warm breezes on my face,
The ripples of water from the paddling pool.

Guy Gibson (10)
Leighfield Primary School

Animal Magnetism

I'm as attracted to you as a brace to a face,
I'm as attracted to you as a shoe to a lace,
I'm as attracted to you as nature to trees,
I'm as attracted to you as a buzz to bees,
I'm as attracted to you as lice to hair,
I'm as attracted to you as a growl to a bear,
I'm as attracted to you as my dad to beer,
I'm as attracted to you as me to a deer,
I'm as attracted to you as a dragon to a lair,
I'm as attracted to you as my sister to a pear,
I'm as attracted to you as a shopper to buying,
I'm as attracted to you as a baby to crying.

Lianne Dalby (10)
Leighfield Primary School

Autumn

A utumn days with the leaves all fallen.
U p in the trees the leaves shiny and brown
T rees getting barer and barer as the days go on
U p in the sky the clouds are grey
M isty mornings when the grass is jewelled
N asty weather is coming.

Louisa Newell & Megan Wright (9)
Leighfield Primary School

Ghosts

G hastly ghosts spook the air. People say we are in despair.
H aunted houses horrify the hills
O verhead lies a ghost, powerful and evil.
S pooky phantoms attack pedestrians.
T ired ghosts lie down to rest.

Daniel Webster & Max Collins (9)
Leighfield Primary School

Classroom

Now that's something new,
His teacher is Mrs McClusted who eats what she's dusted
With old mouldy mustard.
His hamster is yellow and it eats marshmallows,
His bat ate my cat when the cat was quite flat,
In fact, the cat was as flat as a mat.
Well it's not very nice being in a class with him,
Well at least my family's normal except my cat that's green.

Rebecca Higley & Calypso Keightley (9)
Leighfield Primary School

A Pony Poem

A pony poem needs a pony.
A pony that trots,
A pony that stops,
A pony that walks,
A pony that snorts,
A pony that dances,
A pony that prances,
A pony that canters,
A pony that banters,
A pony that eats,
A pony that competes.

Natasha Petty (10)
Leighfield Primary School

Kitty's Miserable Day

Kitty did not want to play,
Not at all today.

Let's play tig?
I am too big to play tig.

Let's play a game of ball,
I don't like that game at all.

Let's climb a tree,
You can, if you like, not me.

Let's play hide-and-seek,
Sorry, but *we played that stupid game last week*.

Well . . . I am going go play with Jane,
Who's promised not to run away again.

Then Kitty, I'll come with you,
Cos you're our dear friend too.

Roshni Makwana (9)
Mellor Community School

Colour Poem

What is blue?
The sky is blue floating up in the air.
What is green?
Green is the grass flying all around.
What is red?
Red is a vocal volcano.
What is yellow?
Yellow is a banana which everybody eats.
What is pink?
The roses are pink with a sweet fragrance.
What is purple?
A pen is purple just like my bed.
What is black?
My trousers are black just like my pen or the colour.
What is brown?
Brown is my cupboard and my bed is brown too.

Raeesa Hussein (9)
Mellor Community School

The Horrors

One of the horrors of mine is sailing away without saying goodbye,
One of the horrors of mine is jumping off a building and falling
                                        to the ground.
One of the horrors of mine is going into the ocean with no air
                                        to breathe.
One of the horrors of mine is being left behind.
One of the horrors of mine is sailing away without saying goodbye.

Bijal Chauhan (10)
Mellor Community School

Lucy, Lucy

Lucy, Lucy you're kind to me,
Lucy, Lucy you're there for me.
Lucy, Lucy you're everywhere,
Lucy, Lucy you're so like me.
Lucy, Lucy you're such a dear it seems,
Like you're here, you're there.
Lucy, Lucy you cheer a mate like me when I'm down,
Lucy, Lucy you're smarter than an owl at night.
Lucy, Lucy I'm there for you,
Lucy, Lucy I'm so like you,
That's why I admire you.

Anesu Rupango (9)
Mellor Community School

My Favourite Colours

Blue is the colour of the tears in my eyes.
Red is the colour of the flames from the fire.
Pink is the colour of the sweet-smelling roses.
Purple is the colour of the fruity violet.
Green is the colour of the juicy Granny Smith apples.
My favourite colours -
Yellow is the colour of shooting and sparkling stars.
White is the colour of the clouds in the sky.
Brown is the colour of my neighbour's fence.
Cream is the colour of the creamy hot chocolate
                              which sparkles in my eyes.
Grey is the colour of the sky before a storm.

Zahra Mussa (9)
Mellor Community School

The Rainbow Colours

(Inspired by 'What is Pink?' by Christina Rosetti)

What is red?
My bed is red shining in the light.
What is green?
The grass is green waving in the light.
What is black?
My hair is black waving across the car.
What is pink?
My shoes are pink sitting on my bed.
What is yellow?
My lemon is yellow sitting on my fish fingers.
What is orange?
An orange of course!

Ameyah Nugent (8)
Mellor Community School

My Colour Poem

What is red?
An apple is red, I eat it before I go to bed.
What is blue?
The sky is blue, I look at it and I look at the moon.
What is green?
Grass is green in the breeze.
What is yellow?
The sun is yellow, it shines in the big sky.
What is brown?
My dog is brown, it woofs all around.
What is white?
My T-shirt is white, I get it dirty all the time.

Anika Bhardwa (8)
Mellor Community School

The Colour Poem

What is red?
A crossing light is red.
What is blue?
The sky is blue.
What is white?
The clouds are white.
What is brown?
Brown is the colour of my eyes.
What is green?
Apples are green.
What is yellow?
The sun is yellow.
What is orange?
Oranges are orange.
What is green?
Grass is green.
What is black?
My hair is black.
What is pink?
Roses are pink.
What is purple?
A coloured pencil is purple.
What is gold?
Treasure is gold.
What is silver?
A projector is silver.

Sahil Dattani (8)
Mellor Community School

My Colourful Poem

What is white?
The moon is white
That shines up bright,
It gives us light,
In the dark, dark night.

What is green?
The leaves are green,
Can easily be seen,
As summer has just been,
To make us keen.

What is red?
The roses are red,
They have been fed,
As the boy has said,
Before going to bed.

What is blue?
The sky is blue,
That gives us a clue,
For what we do,
We should thank you.

Ikra Omar (8)
Mellor Community School

My Colour Poem

What is red?
An apple is red, I eat it before I go to bed.
What is green?
The grass is green, floating all around.
What is yellow?
A light is yellow, shining all around.
What is blue?
The sea is blue, shining in the light.

Hiten Patel (8)
Mellor Community School

The Colour Poem

What is red?
An apple is red, they are tasty it's been said.
What is yellow?
A banana is yellow, it is easy to swallow.
What is green?
A tree is green, it shakes with the windy breeze.
What is blue?
The ocean's blue, it has so many things like fish too.
What is pink?
Grapefruit is pink which is very healthy to eat.

Rahul Somia (9)
Mellor Community School

My Colourful Poem

What is red?
An apple is red,
they are tasty and it's been said.

What is yellow?
A banana is yellow,
when you eat it you swallow it.

What is blue?
Blu-tack is blue,
when you stick it's sticky like glue.

What is green?
Peas are green,
when I eat, I eat in front of the TV screen.

Pratiksha Patel (9)
Mellor Community School

Colour Poem

What is red?
An apple is red,
they are tasty it's been said.

What is yellow?
The sun is yellow,
bright and shiny said that fellow.

What is green?
The grass is green,
short and very lean.

What is blue?
The sky is blue,
light and dark and very clean too.

Neel Somaiya (9)
Mellor Community School

What Am I? Poem

What am I?
I am yellow and mellow,
I am soft and sweet
That you can eat.

What am I?
I grow on trees in hot countries,
I am slightly bent and long
And when you eat me you feel strong.

What am I?
Can you guess?

Umaimah Mussa (8)
Mellor Community School

My Great Poem

Yellow makes me feel sweaty and thirsty.
Red is the dripping blood coming from a dead person.
White makes me feel lonely and unwanted.
Cobalt is the colour of deep blue sea and the sky.
Black makes me feel scared and sad.
Green is the colour of the emerald grass and leaves.
Brown is the colour of the bark of the tree.

Aamir Nur (8)
Mellor Community School

What Is Red?

What is red?
A tomato is red, squeezed on the table.
What is orange?
An orange is orange, hanging on the tree, tilting in the breeze.
What is blue?
The sea is blue, washing up the sand.
What is yellow?
A lemon is yellow, sweet and sour.
What is purple?
A jumper is purple, nice and cosy.

Hamzah Adam (8)
Mellor Community School

Colour Poem

What is white?
The clouds are white, you can't see them at night.
What is brown?
The fence is brown, down on the ground.
What is yellow?
The sun is yellow, shining on a fellow.
What is green?
The grass is green in the midsummer scene.

Maya Mistry (8)
Mellor Community School

Monet's Morning

(Inspiration taken from work by Claude Monet)

Big Ben hiding through the freezing cold fog
Boats smell like smoky chimney tops
Dark, disgusting water crashing against the wall
Banging engines coming alive
Horses crashing their hooves on the solid road
People chatting, rushing to work like a train
London is alive.

Siobhan Robinson (9)
New Swannington Primary School

Monet's Morning

(Inspiration taken from work by Claude Monet)

Big Ben hiding in the freezing cold fog
Boats smell like smoky chimney tops
Park disgusting
Water crashing against the wall
Banging engines coming alive.

Emily Rudin (9)
New Swannington Primary School

Monet's Morning

(Inspiration taken from work by Claude Monet)

Big Ben chimes, striking in the early hours
As the fishermen cast out their lines
Twinkling frost glitters like stars in the midnight sky
Smelly water takes over the crisp morning air
Sleepy builders have worked throughout the night
London is awake.

James Payne (9)
New Swannington Primary School

Monet's Morning

(Inspiration taken from work by Claude Monet)

Seagulls squawking in the cold foggy air
Greyish fog overlapping the morning sky
The taste of the sweet, salty sea
Water runs through the misty air
Rival boats chug to the old crumbling bridge
Reflections of the crystal clear
The blocked up sewer makes the streets of London smell.

Rhys Butler (9)
New Swannington Primary School

Monet's Morning

(Inspiration taken from work by Claude Monet)

Big Ben was hiding in the freezing fog
Women were building a pier for the sailors to get off the boat
Dirty, muddy water splashed furiously against the cracked walls
On the breeze was the smell of dirty seawater.

Kieran Briers (9)
New Swannington Primary School

Monet's Morning

(Inspiration taken from work by Claude Monet)

Big Ben echoes each hour one more chime
Builders working all day, all night with two tea breaks
Misty water running through the streets
People circling through the streets
As I walk past the market people booming
Sickening smells drift out of the slimy sewers
London is alive!

Tania Bodle (10)
New Swannington Primary School

Monet's Morning

(Inspiration taken from work by Claude Monet)

Big Ben's chimes striking in the early hours
As the fishermen cast their lines
Twinkling frost glitters like stars in the midnight sky
Smelly water takes over the crisp morning air
Sleepy builders have worked throughout the night
London is awake.

Jacob Coley (9)
New Swannington Primary School

Monet's Morning

(Inspiration taken from work by Claude Monet)

Big Ben hiding in the freezing cold fog
Boats smell like smoky chimney tops
Dark, disgusting water crashing against the wall
Banging engines coming alive
Horses cracking their hooves on the solid road
People chatting as they wait for the boats
Smell like sewers underneath the water.

Jordan Lester (9)
New Swannington Primary School

Monet's Morning

(Inspiration taken from work by Claude Monet)

Big Ben striking through the streets of London
The frosty autumn trees sparkling near the streets
                              of London riverside
The rumble of engines chugging in the dirty water
The fog, grey and cold air.

Sarah Thomas (9)
New Swannington Primary School

Monet's Morning

(Inspiration taken from work by Claude Monet)

Big Ben stands tall and proud as every hour has the same chime
Completely tired, late night workers sleep at the wet, foggy dawn
Boats racing across the smelly, horrible River Thames
Like drowning men about to die
Water crashes onto the rickety bridge all at the same time
Two best friends stare at the dark green water
And stare whilst they fish cheerfully
Reflections being shown as it stops to a halt in the disgraceful sea
London has awoken and is busy once again.

Sean Lynn (10)
New Swannington Primary School

Monet's Morning

(Inspiration taken from work by Claude Monet)

Frantic frost freezes on the all night trees
Stomach-wrenching sewers make a painful pong for anything
that comes near
Boats drift like a gliding swan as the late night workers stroll
along the deck
Ghastly smoke fills the death-cold air
Revolting water tips over the side of the pebbled path
Bulky Big Ben echoes along the streets of London
London's eyes are now awake.

Libby Birt (10) & Katie White (9)
New Swannington Primary School

Monet's Morning

(Inspiration taken from work by Claude Monet)

Big Ben was hiding in the freezing fog
Workmen were building a pier for the sailors to get off the boats
Dirty, muddy water splashed against the cracked wall
On the breeze was the smell of the dirty seawater.

Lydia Pollard (9)
New Swannington Primary School

Monet's Morning

(Inspiration taken from work by Claude Monet)

Standing high in the sky Big Ben chimes in the morning sky
Boats drifting along the dirty water in the frost
Tired builders work through the night
Greyish fog circles the dull morning sky
Steam boats race to the bridge as smoke fills the air
Glistening fog rests on trees as people stroll past
The water waves crash on the wall
Two people talking, glance into the smelly water
London is awake.

Bethany Tatham (9)
New Swannington Primary School

Monet's Morning

(Inspiration taken from work by Claude Monet)

Frantic frost fills the all night air
Boats drift in and out of tiny waves
Food on boats being passed to the city
Ghostly clouds soon cross the early morning sky
As workers on deck try and try
To catch fish as they stroll along the deck
Big Ben's bong opens London's eye.

Bethany Clarke (10)
New Swannington Primary School

A Spectre Called Hecter

Once was a spectre called Hecter
Whose credit card was a Nectar
He lost his Nectar card
And found it in the yard
He picked it up and inspector.

Toby White (10)
New Swannington Primary School

Monet's Morning

(Inspiration taken from work by Claude Monet)

Standing tall in the frosty air Big Ben chimes his bell
As boats are drifting, engines tossing and turning, boosting
towards the bridge
Beautiful reflections showing that they're proud of what they are
As the workers have been working all night
Dirty water splashes against the solid wall, waves getting smaller
and calmer
Everybody chatting as every word echoes through the old street
London is now awake.

Kia Storer & Elise Baxter (9)
New Swannington Primary School

Monet's Morning

(Inspiration taken from work by Claude Monet)

Big Ben stands tall and proud as every hour has the same chime
Completely tired late night workers sleep at the wet, foggy dawn
Boats racing across the smelly, horrible River Thames
like drowning men about to die
Water crashing onto the rickety bridge
As two best friends stare at the dark green water
as they fish cheerfully
Reflections being shown as it stops at a halt in the sea
London is awake.

Joshua Culpin (9)
New Swannington Primary School

The French Cop

There was a young cop from Paris
He drove a Toyota Yaris
He arrested a cob
That hadn't got a job
And had a daughter called Caris.

Jamie Kerr (10)
New Swannington Primary School

Mum, Please Come Back

Dear Mum and Dad,

How are you doing on your holiday in Spain?
At home it's a bombsite, someone naughty broke into the house.
They fed the dog for some reason.
I am sorry to say they painted the shed,
Then they smashed all of the cups and drank beer out of the mugs,
Then suddenly I saw them filling up the bath
And flooding the place so I ran into the garden.
Then the pond blew up and the frogs and ducks went flying,
I ran into the house
And you won't want to know what happened next.
Anyway, see you when you come back.

Love from Sophie.

PS The frogs and ducks haven't come back yet.

Amelia Cayless (10)
New Swannington Primary School

Monet's Morning
(Inspiration taken from work by Claude Monet)

Strong Big Ben in the distance striking tall in the echoing streets
of London

Frost twinkles like a sword in the trees and roads
As boats zoom along the gliding water
Builders talking and getting tired in the stormy air
Steamy fog overlaps the greyish sky
Reflections standing smart in the smelly water
Dirty water splashes loudly against the wall
London is awake.

Joseph Cayless (9)
New Swannington Primary School

Home Alone

On a dark, dark night
I was woken by the light
I could hear some footsteps
Too loud to be my dad's.

I could see a massive shadow
Too small to be a giant
I went to find my mum and dad
They weren't there and then I was mad.

I hid underneath the covers
Because there wasn't any other
He pulled out a knife
To take away my life.

And when he came to me
I kicked him in the knee
And kicked him down the stairs
I ran down to see him and shaved off all his hair
I threw him in the road and said,
'Don't come back again.'

Sam Moore (10)
New Swannington Primary School

Monet's Morning
(Inspiration taken from work by Claude Monet)

Frantic frost fills the night air
Boats drift in and out of the tiny waves
Food on boats being passed to the city
Ghostly clouds soon cross the early morning sky
As workers on deck try and try to catch fish as they stroll
along the deck
Bulky Big Ben echoes along the streets of London
London's eyes are now wide open.

Sophie Adkins (9)
New Swannington Primary School

Dear Mum

Dear Mum,

While you were out
A china plate cracked on purpose,
The old blue cup that Granpa Joe gave you smashed,
The chandelier fell from the ceiling,
There are big black footprints on your new carpet,
The queen-sized bed fell through the ceiling,
The cat climbed up the curtain and pulled them down,
The rat ate your cushion,
The ants are in the house again,
They're coming out a hole in the floor,
Sasha put her lollipop on the floor
And it is stuck there.

Got to go now,
See you soon,

From Hannah.

Hannah Kelly (10)
New Swannington Primary School

Monet's Morning
(Inspiration taken from work by Claude Monet)

Big Ben stands like a soldier, strong and tall
Shimmering frost shines brightly on the evergreen trees
Seagulls swoop, descending for people's salty chips
Boats crash into water, slowly as they go
Misty fog hover through the sky into the people's faces
Dirty water collides with waves so it goes crash on the wall
London is alive.

Kieran Ridgway & Jordan Wayte (9)
New Swannington Primary School

Dear Manchester United Football Club

Dear Manchester United,

I would love to play
for your great team
because I support you
in every way -
in the hay, even in May.
My favourite players are
Cristiano Ronaldo
and Wayne Rooney.
My whole room
is in Man U stickers
hickers, maybe even knickers
I can't tell you that.
So can I join?
I'll give you a coin.

Thanks for listening.

Your greatest supporter, Chloe Wesley.

Chloe Wesley (10)
New Swannington Primary School

To Mum

To Mum,

The books on the bookshelves are ashes,
The plates are smashed somehow,
The cat is on fire,
The fish is eating cheese,
I know you will flip,
So I am going.

From Ty.

PS: The cat has no fur.

Ty Wardle (10)
New Swannington Primary School

Dear Mum

Dear Mum,

We have a problem,
The roof has started leaking water
And the carpets are drenched.
The puppy is down the chimney, I got him out
And he is all black now.
He has walked into your favourite sock.
Something very scary pulled all of the wallpaper off.
Oh no, the roof has fallen down.
Help Mum, help!

Your loving son Ben.

Rebecca Knight (10)
New Swannington Primary School

Dear Mum

Dear Mum,

You have a great job when I get home,
You have to do my washing and you have to do all of it.
I'm having a great time and my friends are too,
But the food is lovely,
The activities are so cool.
I went to the top of the climbing frame,
I nearly fell but I didn't.
So I will see you when I get home.

Love Mia.

PS: I don't want to come back next year.

Mia Thompson (10)
New Swannington Primary School

Teacher

Dear Teacher,

When you were out the pencil drew on the wall,
Paul went *bang* on the floor,
The door locked,
Clare went into shock,
Oh and,
All the maths book pages suddenly ripped out
And you were taking ages.
The cricket bat hit James round the head,
The cricket ball went through the lab
And hit Mr Johns who was eating a kebab.
Suddenly the lab blew up and out flew the cook,
And now,
I'm sorry, I'm a good girl, I didn't do anything, I promise.

From Jade.

Jasmin Edwards (10)
New Swannington Primary School

The Scout Camp

Dear Mother and Father,

Food's horrible,
Loos are terrible,
Leaders are horrible
And worst of all, the tents are bad.
Have to cook *ourselves!*
Water leaking from the roof.
Please pick me up *now!*

From Luke

PS: Please pick me up, thank you.

Luke Atkinson (10)
New Swannington Primary School

Help Me Mum

Dear Mum,

I am having trouble with my pants
They keep on itching
I think I might have ants
I mean it.

Now I am having trouble with my cape
It seems to be stuck
Probably with tape
Tape that's on my pants.

I have lost one shoe
Oops
I have done a poo!
It's a big one.

Please come and help me
Please Mum
I will make you a cup of tea
Help me!

From Billy.

Brigitte Taylor (10)
New Swannington Primary School

Dear Doctor

Dear Doctor,

My friend kicked me up the bum
So could you help me out?
My mum and dad said I'll be fine
So I went and told my granny
And she pushed me in the bush
So here I am with a thorn up my bum
Please would you help me out?

Yours faithfully

Victoria Campbell.

Victoria Campbell (10)
New Swannington Primary School

When You're Not There

When you're not there,
I'm like . . .
My mum without a book,
A fishing pole without a hook.
Romeo without Juliet,
An owner without their pet.
A gallery without art,
Jam without its tart.
A baby without its mother,
A monk without his brother.
A film without an actor,
An angle without a protractor.
Dorothy without her shoes,
A detective without clues.
Dwarves without Snow White,
A bird without flight.
Franz without Swanilda,
Roald Dahl without Matilda.

Katie Wickham (10)
Leighfield Primary School

Dear Santa

Dear Santa,

Keep off the Fanta,
It really makes you fat.

By the way, this time don't split your trousers
And leave ants.

Oh I forgot to tell you,
You left your pants!

From Charlie Stringer.

Charlie Stringer (10)
New Swannington Primary School

Dear Andy

Dear Andy,

I don't know how the coffee stain got on Mum's new sofa
or how my room became such a mess
I really don't know how the cat turned on the TV
from outside the house
I don't know how some mud prints appeared on
the living room carpet
A crack appeared in Mum's vase and I really don't know how
or how the PC turned on by itself
I think our house is haunted
so I'm going to stay at Val's.

From Callan.

Callan Scott (10)
New Swannington Primary School

Sorry Mr Derin!

Dear Mr Derin,

I'm sorry for that frog in your tea
And for that really big flea,
Oh, when the cup fell it wasn't my fault,
The tap suddenly broke and it wasn't my fault
And then we all shouted,
We all took our jumpers off and tried to stop it,
Even the class next door made it rumble
And they made the glass crumble!

From your favourite student,
Maddi.

Maddi-Rose Harrison (11)
New Swannington Primary School

Dear Teacher

Dear Teacher,

While you were out this is what happened:
The pencils jiggled in and out their pots and drew upon the wall,
The net kind of undid itself and out came the balls,
The chairs came from under the tables and started dancing around,
When they were dancing I was lying on the ground,
The tap turned itself on and flooded up the classroom,
But when I looked at water I really needed the bathroom,
The radio went really loud and turned hip-hop on,
I looked at the sweet box but then they were gone.
I've decorated this letter to make you feel better.

Yours faithfully,
Demi.

PS: I am on my way home.

Demi Demetriou (11)
New Swannington Primary School

Sorry Mum And Dad

Dear Mum and Dad,

I'm sorry about the mess the kitten has been doing,
He squirted the tomato sauce at the new white wall,
He put your lipstick down the toilet with Dad's best underpants,
He ate all the chocolate out the fridge
Then he made a big smelly patch.

From your loving son
Bobby.

Amy Tebbatt (10)
New Swannington Primary School

Dear Mum

Dear Mum,

While you were out.
Out of nowhere my friend's cat pooped on your couch.
Your china plate fell out of the cupboard and smashed.
Your bed fell through the ceiling and fell on my head.
The dog came in and put his muddy footprints all over your
                                          brand new carpet.
The cat clawed over the couch and all the stuffing came out.
The chandelier fell from the ceiling.
I fell off my bed and broke my arm.
I have got to go to the hospital now,
See you soon.

Love Enola.

Enola Curran (10)
New Swannington Primary School

Money Letter

To my dearest mummy,

Please can you send me some money,
I've run out of sweet, sweet honey,
Only kidding,
I've been bidding,
I'm not very good,
I'm covered in mud,
The girl next door makes me laugh,
But I really need a bath.

From your loving son,
David.

PS: I need £100, thanks.

Ellie Summers (10)
New Swannington Primary School

Monet's Morning

(Inspiration taken from work by Claude Monet)

Big Ben echoes, each hour, one more chime
Bulking builders working all day, all night with two tea breaks
Misty water running through the city, sharp smells drifting up
                                                    my red nose

People cycling through the foul-smelling streets
As I walk through the foul-smelling markets people booming
                                                    their sales

Sickening smells drift out of boats' chimneys
Disgusting smells flowing out of sewers.

Lucy Wood (9)
New Swannington Primary School